Freezer Meals: Delicious Gluten Recipes for Make-Ahead Meals Time and Improve Your Health

Copyright © 2014 by Annette Goodman

All rights reserved. No part of this publication may be reproduced, stored in a retrieval system, or transmitted, in any form or by any means, electronic, mechanical, photocopying, recording or otherwise without the prior written permission of the author and the publishers.

All information in this book has been carefully researched and checked for factual accuracy. However, the author and publishers make no warranty, expressed or implied, that the information contained herein is appropriate for every individual, situation or purpose and assume no responsibility for errors and omission. The reader assumes the risk and full responsibility for all actions, and the author will not be held liable for any loss or damage, whether consequential, incidental, and special or otherwise that may result from the information presented in this publication.

Table of Contents:

Chapter 1: Shopping List & Guidelines 5
Freezing Guidelines 6
Freezer Food Safety 8
Chapter 2: Soups 10
Tomato Soup 10
Mexican Chicken Soup 12
Broccoli Soup 14
Vegetable beef soup 16
Chicken Noodle Soup 18
Chapter 3: Dinners 20
Section 1: Chicken 20
Hawaiian Chicken 20
General Tso's Chicken 22
Chicken Curry 24
Santa Fe Chicken 26
Crockpot Chicken with Sweet potato 28
Cacciatore Chicken 30
Cilantro Lime Chicken 32
Section 2: Pork 34
Pork Vindaloo 34
Pork Curry 36
Sweet and Spicy Pork Roast 38
Pork and peppers 40
Green chili pork stew 42
Pineapple Pork 44
Ginger Cranberry Pork Roast 46
Section 3: Beef 48
Broccoli and Beef 48
Pot Roast Beef 50
Beef Stroganoff 52
Beef Stew 54
Garlic Ginger Beef 56
Italian Beef Sandwich 58
Beef Bourguignon 60
Section 4: Lamb 62
Lamb Tangine 62
Lamb Curry 64
Lamb Stew 66
Lamb Stew with Peanut Sauce 68
Lamb Shank 70
Lamb and Fig Stew 72

Slow Roasted Leg of Lamb...74
Chapter 4: Rice and Casseroles..76
Chicken Broccoli Rice Casserole..76
Southwestern Casserole..78
Crockpot Fried Rice...80
Western Beef Casserole..82
Pizza Casserole..84
Squash Casserole..86
Chapter 5: Desserts..88
Molten Choco Lava Cake...88
Orange Cheesecake...90
Low Fat Carrot Cake...92
Peanut Butter Cake...94
Blueberry Crisp..96
Triple Chocolate Brownies..97
Blueberry Cobbler...99
Recommended Reading For You...101
  About The Author...110

My Mailing list: If you would like to receive new Kindle reads on weight loss, wellness, diets, recipes and healthy living for FREE I invite you to my Mailing List. Whenever my new book is out, I set the free period for two days. You will get an e-mail notification and will **be the first to get the book for $0** during its limited promotion.

Why would I do this when it took me countless hours to write these e-books? First of all, that's my way of saying **"thank you"** to my new readers. Second of all – **I want to spread the word about my new books and ideas.** Mind you that **I hate spam and e-mails that come too frequently** - no worries about that.

If you think that's a good idea and are in, just follow this link:
http://eepurl.com/6elQD

Hello! My name is Annette Goodman and I want to thank you for downloading this book. I'm sure that it will help you prepare delicious, healthy and quick meals.

As a person diagnosed with celiac disease I had to soon come up with an efficient strategy that would enable me to maintain my gluten-free diet while handling work, kids, house, sport and all the other areas of my life at the same time. That wasn't easy, and that's why I'm here to give you a helpful hand. Even if you're not diagnosed or gluten intolerant, these recipes will just make you healthier and more energetic.

The best solution is to browse the book, choose a few recipes to your taste and then go shopping a few days ahead with the list I provided in this book not to forget about anything. Then just pick one day of the week when you're not that busy to cook and freeze all the meals in batches for the upcoming week or even the entire month. The best idea is to arrange it with your family or your flat-mates and simply rotate the "cooking days" between all of you. That way your whole family/all your friends will be able to save massive time and money on cooking, shopping and preparing the meals, but you can also do it easily on your own. I use my slow cooker to prepare meals most of time, because the process is healthy and the foods don't lose their nutritional value, minerals and vitamins opposed to many other cooking methods. The slow cooker meals are aromatic, delicate, tempting and just scrumptious! This strategy is also very convenient - you will soon realize how easy and fun it is just to pick one of the meals from your fridge, put into your slow cooker and eat your wholesome meal when you're back home. Of course you can also prepare soups, desserts, lunches and anything that pleases you. If you don't have slow cooker yet, I recommend that you buy it – the best solution for ahead meals is to choose the one that enables you to set the timer for the device to automatically turn on, cook your meal and then turn off.

Before you start, please read the freezing Guidelines and Freezer Food Safety, so that you learn everything that you need for the beginning of your healthy, well-organized and delicious gluten-free journey.

I hope that you like my recipes and I wish you have a great time cooking and, of course, eating them!

Chapter 1: Shopping List & Guidelines

There's a shopping list I prepared to save your precious time:

Produce:

Tomatoes (all varieties), Potatoes (all varieties), Bell peppers (red, green and yellow), Lettuce, Beets, Carrots, Onions (all varieties), All fresh and organic vegetables

Dairy:

Milk (skimmed, whole, condensed), Cheese (except blue cheese), Yogurt

Ice cream, Cottage cheese, Sour cream, Half-and-half

Fruits:

All fresh and organic fruits

Meats, seafood and fish:

Chicken, Turkey, Pork, Ham, Beef, Duck

All types of unadulterated fishes and seafood items

Seasonings and spices:

Salt, Paprika, Black pepper., Cayenne pepper (chili pepper),   White pepper

Gluten-free labeled seasonings and dry herbs (Italian seasoning, rosemary, thyme, oregano etc.), Ginger, Turmeric

Flours:

Rice, Gluten-Free Soy, Potato, Beans, Corn, Bengal gram flour, Nut, Tapioca

Alcoholic beverages:

Sherry, Wine, Rum, Brandy, Vermouth, Cider, Port, Tequila, Gluten free beer, Mead

Pasta and noodles:

Gluten free pasta (from beans, quinoa, brown rice, soy, lentils, potatoes etc.)

Rice noodles

Breads:

Corn bread, Rice bead, Almond bread, Sorghum bread

Miscellaneous:

Eggs, Rice, Baking powder, Corn syrup, Baking soda, Honey, Tofu, Olive oil, Sugar (all varieties), Maple syrup, Tea (preferably non-flavored), Cocoa powder, Gluten free nut butters, Gelatin, Soymilk, Coffee (non-flavored), Cream of tartar, Apple cider vinegar, Gluten free chocolate chips, Pickles, Molasses, Nuts

Legumes:

Beans, Peas, Lentils

Equipment:

Saran wrap, Air tight containers, Gallon size zip lock pouch, Rubber spatula, Freezer friendly aluminum/foil/glass baking pan with lid, Non-stick cooking spray (Gluten Free), Sieve

Freezing Guidelines

1) Double or even treble the amount of ingredients to cook a dish for freezing food in batches. This allows food to be used over a long time.

2) Food should be frozen immediately after cooking and cooling a bit. Freezing the food immediately prevents formation of ice crystals on the food and also stays better after thawing.

3) Never stack packets or jars in the freezer while freezing food. Line them in one layer to freeze and stack only when the food is frozen solid.

4) Soups are better frozen in air tight jars. Saran wraps can be used to warp patties, cover casseroles etc.

5) Always store food by keeping a gap of 2 inches from lid as food tends to swell up and expand on freezing.

6) Always cool food either by placing it over ice cold water or in refrigerator before packing it for freezing.

7) It is always advisable to use the "Fast Freeze" option if available in a freezer.

8) Re-freezing food is possible after thawing (e.g. in case of outage problems), provided it is done within 2 hours of thawing the food, the food is still cold and has ice crystals on it. Keep in mind that you should toss the food if it smells bad, you have any doubts about its safety, or the temperature went above 40 degrees F for more than 2 hours. Never re-freeze warm, completely thawed food!

9) Avoid freezing certain food items like potatoes, eggs, milk, cheese and other dairy products as these foods do not freeze well and tend to become syrupy or get curdled up when frozen. If you want/need to use dairy, use full-fat products – above 40% of fat. Mayonnaise and cream-based puddings are not suitable for freezing at all.

10) If you need to freeze rice, pastas or potatoes – undercook them, as they will need to be reheated later and thus will become a limp mess.

11) If you need to freeze cheese – divide it into parts before freezing, as it

will be very difficult to do it later.

12) Salads and salad greens to be used in salads should not be frozen as they become limp and lose their crispiness after freezing.

13) Always mark the containers with the recipe name and cooking time before freezing for convenience. No food should spend more than 3 months in freezer.

Freezer Food Safety

1) Never keep a cooked food out in room temperature for too long before freezing as that will soon turn stale.

2) Always use freezer ready air tight jars, containers, zip lock bags, aluminum foil or saran wraps to freeze food.

3) Always keep food covered nicely before freezing to ensure safety.

4) Use thawed food immediately that has been left in the room temperature for more than 2 hours.

5) Leftover food should be frozen immediately or within 2 hours to avoid contamination.

6) Do not mix up dairy products, eggs and potatoes with cooked food for freezing as these foods do not freeze well.

7) Never go for air permissible storage jars or wraps for freezing.

8) Foods marked with freezer burns can be used but the portion of the burn should be cut away and discarded before or after cooking the food. Foods with heavy freezer burn marks should not be used for cooking or consumption.

9) Use an appliance thermometer to record the temperature of your refrigerator; it should always be below 40 degrees Fahrenheit.

10) It is always advisable to use the slow thawing method for thawing frozen food, which is by keeping frozen food in refrigerator overnight. For emergency situation however; frozen food can be thawed in microwave oven or by immersing the food containing zip lock bag in ice cold water. However; make sure that the bag is not leaking and that whether it is safe to be used in microwave oven. Don't thaw foods in warm room temperatures as they will be prone to contamination - especially in a warm climate.

Chapter 2: Soups

Tomato Soup

Servings: 8 to 12 (freezing)

Preparation Time: 15 minutes

Cooking Time: 4 hours

Ingredients-

- 2 lbs. (~910 g) of fresh or canned tomatoes
- 1/2 cup of white wine
- 1/2 of a medium sized onion, roughly chopped
- 2-3/4th cup of vegetable broth
- 2/3rd cup of unsweetened almond milk-
- 2 teaspoons of dried basil
- 2 tablespoons of tomato paste
- ½ teaspoon of ground cumin
- 1/4th teaspoon of ground black pepper (better if freshly ground)
- 1 teaspoon of Salt

(Double the quantities of ingredients for freezing)

Method of preparation:

1) Cut the fresh tomatoes in half and then core them. Put tomatoes in crock pot one by one after coring them. Take a medium sized onion. Cut the onion in half and peel one of the halves. Chop the peeled onion half roughly and then add those to the cored tomatoes in the crock pot. Once done, add to the tomatoes and the onion the white wine, vegetable broth, tomato paste, dried basil, ground cumin, salt and black pepper. Once everything is added, give a light stir to the mixture and then cover the crock pot with its lid.

2) Cook the mixture lid on for 4 hours. Once the cooking time elapses, pour the mixture into a large bowl and let it sit for a few minutes so as to cool it. It is essential that the mixture cools down before blending it or else it may blow up. Once completely cooled, pour the mixture into the blender and blend it till it attends a fine texture.

3) Once the mixture is thoroughly blended, take a big bowl and place a large strainer over it. Pour the soup slowly through the strainer to collect the fine soup without any extra pulp.

4) This is the ideal time for freezing the soup. For that, pour the cooled soup into an air-tight jar and pop it into the freezer.

5) To serve the soup, thaw the frozen soup and then add the unsweetened almond milk to the soup. Stir a bit and heat up the soup on low heat without boiling it.

6) Once you are done heating the soup, serve it in individual soup bowls with some gluten free crackers.

Freezing Instructions:

1) After preparing the soup, cool it immediately by placing the bowl of soup over ice bath or ice water. Once cooled, pour into an air tight container and pop immediately into the freezer.

Thawing Instructions:

1) For thawing the tomato soup that you have strained and frozen, remove the soup container from the freezer and place it in the refrigerator overnight.

2) A great way to store and freeze tomato paste without keeping it in the open container is to fill each of the compartments of an ice cube tray with 1 tablespoon of the tomato paste. Keep the ice tray in freezer and use the tomato paste cubes as and when required.

Mexican Chicken Soup

Servings: 6

Preparation Time: 30 minutes

Cooking Time: 6-8 hours

Ingredients:

- 3 cups of chicken, cut into 1 inch (2.5 cm) sized cubes
- 6 cups of chicken stock
- 1 cup of tomato juice
- 1/5th cup of red onion, roughly diced
- ½ cup of chopped Roma tomatoes
- ½ cup of carrot, peeled and finely diced
- 1 teaspoon of coriander powder
- 4 teaspoons of minced garlic
- ½ cup of fresh cilantro, roughly chopped
- 1 teaspoon of cumin powder
- 2 tablespoons of freshly squeezed lime juice
- 1 teaspoon of chili powder
- 2 teaspoons of sea salt

Cooking procedure:

1) To start with, take the chicken and cut it into 1 inch sized cubes. Now place it aside in a large bowl. Now take a red onion and cut in half. Peel off the skin of the onion halves and then dice those roughly so that you get 1/5th cup worth of diced onions. Next, take the Roma tomatoes and chop those to get ½ cup worth of chopped tomatoes.

2) Next, take the carrots and wash those nicely under running water. Scrub the carrots a bit to get rid of grime and dirt. Once done, peel the carrots and then dice those finely. Finally, chop the fresh corianders and set aside all the chopped vegetables.

3) Once you are done with the vegetables, take a lime and squeeze out 2 tablespoons worth of juice from it. Now take a large enough freezer compatible air-tight container and put the chicken cubes in it. Top the chicken cubes with the chopped vegetables like tomatoes, coriander, carrots and onion. Add the fresh lime juice and the minced garlic.

4) Continue with adding the spices like ground cumin, chili powder, coriander powder and sea salt. Once everything is added, give a nice toss to the mixture with a ladle.

5) Finally, pour the tomato juice and chicken stock all over the chicken and the vegetables. Toss everything up once again to mix nicely and then close the lid of the container tightly.

6) Slid the container into the freezer to freeze the mixture. Once ready to serve the soup, take the container out of the freezer and place it in the refrigerator overnight to thaw.

7) Once the soup is thawed, pour it as it is into a slow cooker and slow cook the soup for 6-8 hours before serving. Serve in individual serving bowls to enjoy it warm.

Freezing Instructions:

1) Cool the soup immediately after cooking to prevent bacterial attack by placing the soup bowl over chilled water and then pop it into freezer after storing into an air tight container.

Thawing Instructions:

1) Take out the air tight container of the soup from the freezer and let thaw in the refrigerator for a few hours. Transfer it to the sink and let sit under cold running water to thaw completely.

Broccoli Soup

Servings: 6

Preparation Time: 15 minutes

Cooking Time: 3-6 hours

Ingredients:

- 10 cups of broccoli florets, cut into small pieces
- 10 cups of low sodium chicken broth
- 4 cloves of garlic, minced
- 3/4th cup of unsalted butter
- 1 cup of heavy cream
- 3 cups of diced onion (yellow onion)
- 4 oz. (112 g) of fresh parmesan cheese, finely shredded
- 4×12 oz. (680 ml) cans of evaporated milk
- 1/4th teaspoon of dried thyme
- 24 oz. (680 g) of sharp cheddar cheese, finely shredded
- Salt, to taste
- Freshly ground black pepper, to taste

Method of preparation:

1) Take the broccoli and rinse it properly under running water. Cut the broccoli into small sized florets and then set it aside. Cut and mince the garlic. Follow that by peeling and chopping the yellow onion.

2) Now take a medium sized skillet and place it on the stove. Warm the skillet gently and drop in the butter. Once the butter melts, add the chopped onions and sauté them until they turn translucent and become softer. Next, add the minced garlic to the onion and season the mixture with salt and black pepper. Cook the mixture stirring it constantly for 2

minutes and then drop it into the slow cooker.

3) Add the broccoli florets, thyme and the chicken stock to the onion and garlic mixture. Put the lid on the slow cooker and let the soup cook for 6 hours on low. You can also speed up the process by setting the slow cooker on high to cook the soup for 3 hours.

4) Once the soup is cooked, open the lid of the slow cooker and transfer the mixture to a bowl to cool it down. You can then store the soup in an air tight freezer friendly container or bag and insert it into your freezer. The soup will stay good for as long as 2 months, depending on the quality of the container you are using.

5) To serve the soup after freezing it, remove the frozen soup from the freezer and let it stand in the refrigerator for 24 hours. Once thawed, pour the soup into a skillet and add the evaporated milk to it. Stir until the soup thickens up a bit and then add-in the heavy cream, grated parmesan and cheddar cheese. Season the soup with salt and pepper if required and serve hot.

Freezing Instruction:

1) It is best to freeze soup in airtight containers after immediately cooling it after cooking.

Thawing Instructions:

1) Either thaw the soup completely by placing the container in the refrigerator for 12 hours or more or place it under cold running water to thaw.

Vegetable beef soup

Servings: 6-7

Preparation time: 20-25 minutes

Cooking time: 8 hours

Ingredients:

2 lbs. (907 g) of beef stew meat

1-3/4th cup of diced tomatoes

1 cup of chopped celery

1 medium sized red onion, peeled and chopped

3 large potatoes

1-3/4th cup of gluten free beef broth

1 cup of chopped carrots

1 medium sized bay leaf

3 cups of water

1 tablespoon of gluten free dried parsley

A pinch of ground black pepper

1 teaspoon of dried basil

Method of preparation:
1) To prepare the dish, cut the beef stew pieces into 1 inch sized pieces and then season those nicely with salt and ground black pepper. Then cut and chop the veggies as provided in the list of ingredients list and then throw them into a gallon zip lock pouch, except for the potatoes.

2) Take a skillet and place it over medium heat. Grease the skillet with 2-3 tablespoons of cooking oil and dump the beef in the skillet. Brown the beef and then transfer it to a bowl. Put the bowl to refrigerator to cool down the beef and then put the cooled beef into a gallon zip lock bag.

3) Add the vegetables, except the tomatoes and the potatoes to the beef and then add the bay leaf, sugar, dried basil and black pepper to the beef. Close the bag and label it. Sore the bag in freezer until ready to use.

4) When ready to use, thaw the bag and then tip the beef and vegetable mixture into the slow cooker. Add the tomatoes, potatoes, water and beef broth to the mixture and cook the soup on low for 6 to 8 hours or until the vegetables and beef turn soft.

5) Use the soup immediately and store the left over in zip lock bags or a freezer friendly container. Freeze the soup and reheat it in slow cooker for 1-2 hours as needed.

Freezing instructions:

1) To freeze the raw soup, store the ingredients in a gallon zip lock bag after the beef cools down in the refrigerator. Mark the bag and freeze until necessary.

2) To freeze the cooked soup, store the soup in an air tight freezer container and

Thawing instructions:

1) To thaw the bag or container of raw or cooked soup, remove it from the freezer and place in refrigerator for 12 hours. Use the contents within an hour of thawing or freeze again.

Chicken Noodle Soup

Servings: 8

Preparation time: 15-20 minutes

Cooking time: 5-6 hours

Ingredients:

2 cups of cooked chicken

5 cups of chicken broth (gluten free)

½ cup of sliced green onion

1 1/3rd cup of gluten free cream of chicken soup

2 cups of corn

½ cup of chopped celery

½ cup of diced onions

1 ½ cups of gluten free noodles

½ cup of chopped carrots

Salt, to taste

Crushed black pepper, to taste

Method of preparation:
1) Peel and chop the vegetables as stated in the list of ingredients and then tip them into a gallon zip lock pouch. Add the chicken broth, salt and black pepper to the chicken and lock the bag by pushing out as much air as possible.

2) Freeze the bag by first labeling, until you are ready to use and do not add the cooked chicken and noodles to the mixture while preparing to freeze. Once ready to use, tip the thawed mixture into a slow cooker and cook on low for 5-6 hours. Add the chicken and noodles 1 hour prior to serving and cook for another 1 hour. Serve hot.

Freezing instructions:

1) To freeze the bag, place all the ingredients in a marked zip lock bag, except the noodles and the cooked chicken.

Thawing instructions:

1) Take out the bag of soup from freezer and place in refrigerator overnight or place it below running water to thaw it completely if you don't find the time to thaw it completely in the refrigerator.

Chapter 3: Dinners

Section 1: Chicken

Hawaiian Chicken

Servings: 3-4

Preparation Time: 20-25 minutes

Cooking Time: 8 hours

Ingredients:

- 3-4 frozen chicken breasts (boneless and skinless)
- 1 large green bell pepper, deseeded and cut into chunks
- 2 cups of pineapple chunks
- 1 onion, peeled and cut into chunks
- 1 heaping tablespoon of orange marmalade
- 3 tablespoons of gluten free soy sauce
- 1 large red bell pepper, deseeded and cut into chunks
- 1/4th teaspoon of paprika
- 1/2 teaspoon of salt

Method of preparation:

1) Start by rinsing the vegetables and the fruits. Now cut the green and red bell peppers in half and extract the seeds. Cut the bell peppers into medium sized square chunks. Cut the pineapple into chunks as well and retain a bit of their juices. Finally cut the onion into chunks after peeling off its skin.

2) Now take a large freezer friendly air tight zip lock pouch and load the fruits, vegetables and the chicken breasts into it. Add the gluten free

soy sauce, salt, paprika and the orange marmalade to it. Close the zip lock bag properly and then shake and toss the ingredients in it to mix them thoroughly with the seasonings and the orange marmalade.

3) Leave the bag in the freezer until you are ready to cook the Hawaiian chicken and take it out of the freezer the night before you plan to cook the chicken dish. Thaw the frozen mixture and then dump the entire mixture into your slow cooker. Set the cooker on low and allow the chicken to cook for 8 long hours.

4) Once ready with the chicken, take out the chicken breasts from the slow cooker and shred them either with your hands or two forks. Dump the shredded chicken back in the slow cooker and warm it through by cooking it on low. Serve hot over warm rice.

Freezing Instructions:

1) Pack the chicken in a container and pop in the refrigerator to cool it down after cooking. Place a lid loosely over it to avoid contamination. Once cooled, pack in sealable pouches and freeze.

Thawing Instructions:

1) Remove the zip lock bag from your freezer the night before you plan to cook it. Place the bag in the refrigerator and let the mixture thaw overnight in your refrigerator. Letting the mixture to thaw overnight will no more require you to stir the mixture midway while cooking it.

General Tso's Chicken

Servings: 4

Preparation Time: 10 minutes

Cooking Time: 5-6 hours

Ingredients:

- 1 lb. (455 g) of skinless and boneless chicken breasts, cut into 1 inch sized cubes
- 2 cups of stir fry vegetables
- 1 teaspoon of ground ginger
- 1/2 teaspoon of crushed red pepper flakes
- 3 tablespoon of brown sugar
- 2 tablespoons of gluten free soy sauce
- 4 tablespoons of minced garlic

Method of preparation:

1) Dump the stir fried vegetables into a re-sealable zip lock pouch and insert the bag into the freezer. Now take the chicken breasts and skin those if not already skinned. Once you have completed removing the skin, cut the chicken breasts into 1 inch sized cubes.

2) Now mix the brown sugar, soy sauce, ground ginger, minced garlic and red pepper flakes together. Once ready, pour the mixture over the chicken breasts. Dump the entire thing into another freezer specific zip lock pouch and then close the lock properly to avoid the juices from leaking and running out, thereby flooding your entire freezer. Once done, toss the contents of the bag nicely so as to mix the sauce and other spices with the chicken. Put the bag of chicken into the freezer as well.

3) Once ready to cook, thaw the chicken and vegetables and then dump the chicken in your slow cooker. Cook on slow for 5-6 hours. Then add the thawed vegetables, cook for another hour and serve hot over rice.

Freezing Instructions:

1) It is always better to store and freeze chicken in air tight containers or sealable bags.

Thawing Instructions:

1) Once ready to cook the dish, remove chicken from freezer and thaw it overnight in refrigerator. Thaw the stir fried vegetables for a few hours before cooking the batch in the slow cooker.

Chicken Curry

Servings: 4

Preparation Time: 10-15 minutes

Cooking Time: 8-9 hours

Ingredients:

6 skinless and boneless chicken breasts

8 fresh green onions, roughly chopped

2 cups of gluten free cream of chicken soup

2 tablespoons of curry powder

1 cup of dry cooking sherry

Salt, to taste

½ cup of butter

Black pepper, to taste

Method of preparation:

1) Take the chicken and rinse it thoroughly. Cut off any extra fat and then drop the chicken beast pieces into a zip lock pouch. Now rinse and chop the green onions and dump those into the bag with the chicken as well.
2) Add the remaining ingredients like sherry, cream of chicken soup and curry powder to the chicken. Finally, season the chicken with black pepper and salt and then lock the bag.
3) Toss the bag nicely to coat the chicken with the rest of the ingredients and then keep the bag in the freezer until you want to cook the dish. To cook, thaw the frozen chicken completely. Add the butter to the slow cooker and then dump the chicken in it. Cook for 8-9 hours on low or until the chicken reaches your desired softness. Once done, serve over warm rice.

Freezing Instructions:

1) Freeze the raw chicken and the vegetables by storing them according to portion size in zip lock pouches.

Thawing Instructions:

1) Place the pouch in refrigerator as and when required and let it thaw for 12 hours before use. Once thawed, use within 2 days.

Santa Fe Chicken

Servings: 6-7

Preparation time: 20-25 minutes

Cooking time: 8 hours

Ingredients:

7 large chicken breasts

1 1/4th cup of diced tomatoes (avoid canned varieties)

1 shack of corn

2 cups of chili beans

1-2 tablespoons of chopped green chilies

1/2 teaspoon of paprika

1 medium sized onion, peeled and chopped

1/2 teaspoon of salt

1 teaspoon of ground cumin

Method of preparation:

1) Keep the chili beans soaked in water overnight. Next morning, take the corn shack and rinse it. Remove the corn kernels with the help of a knife and then cut the onion, green chilies and tomatoes. Keep everything mixed in a large bowl.

2) Add the paprika powder and the ground cumin. Mix everything up thoroughly and then take a saran wrap. Grease the saran wrap lightly with oil and then put the chicken breasts in it. Spoon out the corn and beans mixture over the chicken and then pack the entire parcel in a gallon zip lock pouch.

3) To cook the chicken, thaw it completely and then dump the entire

mixture into your slow cooker. Season with salt and give a light stir to mix. Cook the chicken on high for 4-5 hours or on low for 7-8 hours. Serve with baked potatoes.

Freezing instructions:
1) Place the chicken breasts and vegetables in a saran wrap and wrap the mixture properly, so that it becomes air tight. Insert the pack into a zip lock pouch and place it in freezer to freeze.

Thawing instructions:
1) To thaw the chicken, remove the saran wrap parcel from the gallon pouch and keep it in the refrigerator overnight.

Crockpot Chicken with Sweet potato

Servings: 4

Preparation time: 10-15 minutes

Cooking time: 6 hours

Ingredients:

2 large sweet potatoes, peeled and chopped

½ cup of chopped red onions

1 lb. (455 g) of boneless and skinless chicken breasts, cut into 1 inch sized cubes

1 cup of unsweetened apple sauce

2 teaspoons of curry powder

2 large cloves of garlic, peeled and minced

1/2 teaspoon of ground ginger

2 teaspoons of apple cider vinegar

Salt, to taste

Freshly ground black pepper

Method of preparation:
1) Cut the chicken into cubes and dump it into a gallon size freezer friendly bag. Add the ground ginger, chopped onion and garlic cloves to the chicken. At the remaining ingredients instead of the sweet potatoes to the chicken. Lock the zip lock bag and insert it into the refrigerator.

2) Let the bag stay in the refrigerator for as long as you are not ready to use it. Once ready to use, thaw the bag and tip the thawed mixture into the slow cooker. Now peel and cut the sweet potatoes into chunks and add the chunks to the chicken. Cook the chicken on low for 6-8 hours or until the chicken reaches the desired tenderness. Once done, serve warm over warm rice.

Freezing instructions:

1) It is better to use a zip lock pouch to freeze the food.

Thawing instructions:

1) To thaw the bag of chicken, place it in the refrigerator for 12 hours.

Cacciatore Chicken

Servings: 6-8

Preparation time: 5-10 minutes

Cooking time: 8 hours

Ingredients:

8 skinless and boneless chicken breasts

1/2 of large onion, peeled and chopped

3 ½ cup of crushed tomatoes

4 tablespoons of crushed fresh herbs (basil and parsley)

1/2 red bell pepper, seeded and cut into thin strips

1 bay leaf

1/2 green bell pepper, seeded and cut into thin strips

1/2 teaspoon of gluten free dried oregano

Salt, to taste

Freshly ground black pepper, to taste

Method of preparation:

1) Cut off the skin and excess fat from chicken breasts and tip the chicken into a freezer compatible zip lock gallon bag. Add the green and red pepper strips and the crushed tomatoes to the chicken. Add the dried oregano, fresh herbs, bay leaf, chopped onions, salt and black pepper to the chicken.

2) Lock the pouch while forcing out maximum air from it and then insert the bag into the freezer. When ready to cook, thaw the bag and dump the thawed mixture into the slow cooker. Let the chicken cook on low for 8 hours or on high for 4 hours. Once ready, serve warm over rice or pasta and refreeze the leftover in the same way as before.

Freezing instructions:
1) To freeze the cooked or uncooked chicken, store it in a zip lock bag or container and freeze. This will stay good for as long as 2-3 months in a completely frozen form.

Thawing instructions:
1) Place the frozen bag in fridge for as long as 12 hours for complete thawing.

Cilantro Lime Chicken

Servings: 4-5

Preparation time: 5 minutes

Cooking time: 4 hours

Ingredients:

1½ cups of boneless and skinless chicken breasts

2 cups of fresh or frozen corns (gluten free if canned)

Juice from 2 big limes

1 can of black beans (gluten free)

1 cup of chopped fresh cilantro

2 large cloves of garlic, peeled and minced

1 teaspoon of cumin

1/2 of a large red onion, peeled and chopped

Salt, to taste

Ground black pepper, to taste

Method of preparation:
1) Remove the juice from 2 limes and chop the onion. Drop the chicken breasts in a zip lock bag designed to be used in freezer and then add the chopped onion, black beans, corns, lime juice, cilantro, cumin, cloves of garlic, salt and black pepper.

2) Once everything is packed into the bag, seal it and then lay it flat in the freezer to freeze. Once ready to use, thaw the bag completely in the refrigerator. Once thawed, tip the entire content of the bag in the slow cooker and then cook it covered on high for 4 hours or on low for 6-8 hours or until the chicken reaches the desired consistency.

3) The chicken may also be shredded 30 minutes prior to serving the dish. Once ready, serve the chicken over rice or as a filing for gluten free tortilla wraps. The chicken may also be frozen at this point.

Freezing instructions:

1) To freeze the cooked chicken, cool it immediately after cooking by placing it in the refrigerator. Once cooled, pack the chicken in air tight container or zip lock bag and freeze flat in the freezer.

Thawing instructions:

1) Place the bag of frozen chicken in the refrigerator overnight to thaw the chicken completely and safely.

Section 2: Pork

Pork Vindaloo

Servings: 4-6

Preparation Time: 30 minutes

Cooking Time: 8-10 hours

Ingredients:

2 lbs. (~910 g) of pork shoulder or pork loin, cut into small cubes

12 medium sized cloves of garlic, peeled

1 large red onion, peeled and cut into cubes

2 cups of diced tomatoes

3 tablespoons of grainy mustard

One 3 inch rhizome of ginger, grate

1/2 cup of gluten free apple cider vinegar

1 ½ tablespoons of cardamom powder

1 medium sized stick of cinnamon

4 tablespoons of olive oil

A pinch of red pepper flakes

2 large red bell peppers, deseeded and julienned

1 1/2 teaspoon of cumin powder

2 tablespoons of curry powder

1/2 teaspoon of ground cloves

1 teaspoon of sea salt

Method of preparation:
1) Put the garlic, ginger, spices (except the cinnamon stick), apple cider vinegar and olive oil into a grinder and grind the mixture into fine paste. If the paste is too tight, add a bit of water or oil to make it workable.

Now cut the pork shoulder or pork loin into medium sized pieces and pour the spice mixture over the pork. Rub the spice mixture all over the pork and pack in a zip lock bag.

2) Cut the vegetables (except tomatoes) and tip those into the bag of pork. Seal the gallon zip lock bag and store it in the freezer until you plan to cook it. To cook the pork vindaloo, thaw the pork and vegetables mixture completely and then dump it all in your slow cooker.

3) Finally cut the tomatoes and add those to the rest of the ingredients. Add the cinnamon stick and season the pork with a bit of salt. Set the slow cooker on low and cook the pork vindaloo for 7-8 hours, until it reaches your desired softness. Serve over rice with broccoli, bell peppers or any other vegetable of your choice.

Freezing Instructions:

1) Pack the recommended ingredients in zip lock bags or air-tight jars and place in freezer to freeze.

Thawing Instructions:

1) To thaw the bag of pork vindaloo, transfer it your refrigerator and let sit there for 12 hours for completely thawing it.

Pork Curry

Servings: 4-6

Preparation Time: 20-30 minutes

Cooking Time: 7-8 hours

Ingredients:

2 lbs. (~910 g) of pork loin, boneless

1 clove of garlic

1 large onion, peeled and diced

2 tablespoons of gluten free chicken stock or water

4 tablespoons of chopped prunes or raisins

1 raw apple, peeled and diced

2 tablespoons of corn starch/ corn flour (gluten free)

A pinch of ground cinnamon

1 cup of freshly squeezed orange juice (avoid bottled or canned juice)

1/2 teaspoon of ground ginger

2 teaspoons of curry powder

Salt, to taste

Method of preparation:
1) Cut the boneless pork loin into 1 inch sized cubes. Then take the vegetables and cut those as mentioned. Pack the pork pieces and vegetables (except apple) into a gallon zip lock pouch. Add the spices as well and then pack the bag by sealing it tightly. Pop into the freezer for freezing.
2) Place the zip lock pouch in freezer and let it thaw in the refrigerator when ready to cook the dish. Once done thawing, tip the mixture into slow cooker. Cut the apple and add it to the pork in the slow cooker.

Pour orange juice over the mixture and let the pork cook on low for 7-8 hours.

3) Dissolve the corn flour in the chicken stock and then pour the mixture into the crock pot. Give a light stir and cook for another 30 minutes on high. Sprinkle the prunes or raisins on top to serve.

Freezing Instructions:

1) Pack the ingredients in air-tight containers or freezer bag to freeze.

Thawing Instructions:

1) Keep the bag of pork in your refrigerator for at least 12 hours to thaw the bag completely. However; keeping it in the refrigerator for a few hours would also thaw the contents of the bag, if not completely. Alternatively, transfer the frozen meat to containers or a plate to thaw.

Sweet and Spicy Pork Roast

Servings: 10

Preparation Time: 10-15 minutes

Cooking Time: 6-8 hours

Ingredients:

5 lbs. (~2.3 kg) of pork roast

1 cup of brown sugar

1 tablespoon of onion powder

2 tablespoons of vegetable oil

1 teaspoon of sage

3 teaspoons of garlic powder

1 teaspoon of cayenne pepper

1 tablespoon of salt

1 tablespoon of ground mustard

1 tablespoon of paprika

3 teaspoons of black pepper powder

Method of preparation:
1) Rinse and prepare the pork roast and then mix the garlic powder, cayenne pepper powder, sage, ground mustard, onion powder, salt, black pepper powder, paprika and vegetable oil with the brown sugar. Stir well to mix and then rub the mixture all over the pork roast.
2) Divide the pork mixture into gallon zip lock bags and freeze until ready to use. Thaw the mixture completely by placing it into the refrigerator for 12 hours and cook the entire thing in slow cooker on low for 6-8 hours.

Freezing Instructions:

1) Zip lock bags and containers are ideal for freezing food.

Thawing Instructions:

1) Place in refrigerator for 12 hours to thaw completely. However; keeping the bag in the refrigerator for a few hours would also thaw the contents of the bag, if not completely.

Pork and peppers

Servings: 4-6

Preparation time: 15-20 minutes

Cooking time: 6-8 hours

Ingredients:

4-6 pork chops

1 large red bell pepper, deseeded and cut into cubes

1 large yellow bell pepper, deseeded and cut into cubes

2 cups of diced red tomatoes

1 medium sized red onion, peeled and diced

3 tablespoons of gluten free Worcestershire sauce

2 large cloves of garlic, minced

1/2 teaspoon of dried thyme (gluten free)

Salt, to taste

Ground black pepper, to taste

Method of preparation:

1) Take the pork chops in a plate and season those nicely with salt and black pepper and then drop them into a re-sealable gallon pouch. Deseed and cut the bell peppers into small pieces and then throw those into the bag with the pork chops.

2) Add the onion pieces and the diced red tomatoes and then add the dried thyme, Worcestershire sauce and the minced garlic. Once everything has been loaded into the bag, seal the pouch and give a nice toss to the ingredients to mix the herbs, seasonings and sauces with the vegetables and pork.

3) Keep the bag in your freezer and then take it out to thaw once you are ready to cook the pork. Thaw the mixture and then place the mixture into your slow cooker. Cook the pork for 6-8 hours on low until you get the desired tenderness. If you haven't thawed the mixture completely, cook the mixture on low for 8-10 hours.

Freezing instructions:
1) Use a high quality freezer compatible zip lock bag to store the vegetables and pork and place the bag in the freezer to freeze the food.

Thawing instructions:
1) Remove the gallon zip lock pouch from the freezer and let it stand in refrigerator overnight or for 12 hours to thaw the mixture.

Green chili pork stew

Servings: 6

Preparation time: 10 minutes

Cooking time: 7-8 hours

Ingredients:

2 lbs. (~908 g) of boneless pork loin roast, fat removed

1 cup of roughly chopped onion

2 tablespoons of chopped fresh jalapeño

2 tablespoons of corn flour (or any gluten free flour)

1 1/4th cup of diced red tomatoes

1 cup of green chilies

1/2 teaspoon of garlic powder

2 tablespoons of olive oil

1/2 cup of homemade gluten free chicken broth

1 tablespoon of cumin powder

Salt, to taste

Freshly ground black pepper, to taste

Method of preparation:

1) Take the pork loin roast and trim off excess fat from it. Cut the pork into small 2 inch sized pieces and then throw them into a good quality plastic re-sealable zip lock pouch. Add the chopped onions, green chilies, jalapeño, diced tomatoes, garlic powder, salt, black pepper and cumin powder to the pork. Seal the bag tightly and then toss everything up nicely to coat. Toss the bag of pork in the freezer and let it stand there while you do something else.

2) Once ready to cook, thaw the bag in the refrigerator. Now set your slow

cooker on slow and pour the oil into it. Once the oil heats up, throw everything contained in the bag into the slow cooker. Let the meat cook on low for 7-8 hours and then 1/2 an hour prior to serving, open the slow cooker and take out a bit of the juices.

3) Dissolve the corn flour in the juices and then pour the mixture into the slow cooker. Put the lid back and cook for another half an hour. Serve hot over rice.

Freezing instructions:
1) Tip the pork and the rest of the suggested ingredients in an air tight bag and then mark the bag with the recipe name. flatten out the bag and place it in the freezer to freeze; however do not stack it below other packets while freezing. Stacking should be done only after the food is frozen solid.

Thawing instructions:
1) To thaw the pork, put the bag into the refrigerator from the freezer and let it sit there overnight.

Pineapple Pork

Servings: 2-3

Preparation time: 5-10 minutes

Cooking time: 4-9 hours

Ingredients:

1.5 lbs. (~680 g) of cubed pork tenderloin pork loin

20 oz. (~570 g) of crushed pineapple (gluten free, preferably fresh)

1/2 of a medium sized onion chopped

1/2 cup of gluten free packaged apple juice or fresh apple juice

1 teaspoon of gluten free Italian seasoning

1/2 of a red pepper, chopped

3 tablespoons of corn starch

2 tablespoons of gluten free brown sugar

1/2 teaspoon of kosher salt

1/2 teaspoon of freshly ground black pepper

Method of preparation:

1) Place a gallon size zip lock over the kitchen counter or table and drop the pork cubes in it. Chop the onion and pepper and add those to the pork. Follow that by adding the brown sugar, corn starch, kosher salt, Italian seasoning and freshly ground black pepper to the meat.

2) Now close the zip lock bag and give a nice shake to mix up the herbs and seasonings with the meat. Finally, add in the apple juice to the meat and freeze on freezer until you plan to use it.

3) To use the meat, thaw it and then dump the thawed mixture into the slow cooker. Add the crushed pineapples and cook on low for 7-9 hours or on high for 4-6 hours. Server warm over rice.

Freezing instructions:

1) Mix everything up in a zip lock gallon bag, except for the pineapple and freeze.

Thawing instructions:
1) The bag should ideally be placed in the refrigerator for 24 hours prior to cooking.

Ginger Cranberry Pork Roast

Servings: 6-8

Preparation time: 10-15 minutes

Cooking time: 4-6 hours

Ingredients:

2 whole pork roasts

2 tablespoons of honey or maple syrup

12 oz. (~340 g) of fresh cranberries

½ cup of water

2 tablespoons of arrowroot powder

1 cup of peeled and sliced ginger

Method of preparation:

1) Slice the ginger and then drop the pork roast into a freezer bag or container which is air tight. Top the pork with the cranberries, sliced ginger and honey. Once everything is added, lock the bag or container and give a nice shake or toss to the mixture to combine the ingredients with the pork. Once done, place in freezer to freeze.

2) Remove the bag of pork from the freezer and let it sit in the refrigerator prior to cooking. Once thawed, dump the pork mixture into the slow cooker and pour 1/2 cup of water over the mixture.

3) Stir the mixture slightly to mix the water with the rest of the ingredients and then let it cool for 4-6 hours on low or until the pork is thoroughly cooked. Dissolve the arrowroot powder in the juices to thicken the juice and then serve by slicing the pork and pouring the cranberry sauce over the pork slices.

Freezing instructions:
1) It is best to use a zip lock bag or air right jar to store the meat for freezing.

Thawing instructions:
1) The container or bag can be either placed in the refrigerator for 24 hours to thaw the meat completely or placed under running water at room temperature after refrigerating for a few hours in the fridge.

Section 3: Beef

Broccoli and Beef

Servings: 4-5

Preparation Time: 15-20 minutes

Cooking Time: 6-8 hours

Ingredients:

2 lbs. (~908 g) of beef strips

2-3 tablespoons of cooking oil

8 cups of broccoli florets

1 cup of brown sugar

2 cups of gluten free beef broth

6 large cloves of garlic, peeled and minced

1 cup of gluten free soy sauce

1 tablespoon of cornstarch

Method of preparation:
1) Cut the beef into thin strips and set them aside. Take a skillet and place it over medium heat. Heat up the cooking oil in the skillet and once hot, dump the beef strips into the skillet to fry. Once browned nicely on all sides, remove from skillet and set aside.
2) Take 6 cloves of garlic, peel and mince those. Take minced garlic worth of 3 garlic cloves and add the soy sauce, beef broth and brown sugar to it. Stir to mix well and make a sauce. Keep aside.
3) Take a large gallon sized freezer-specific zip lock bag and put the browned beef strips into it. Add the broccoli florets and the remaining minced garlic to it. Finally, add the prepared sauce. Seal the bag and toss it to mix the contents of the bag nicely with the sauce. Label and freeze until ready to use.

4) To cook the beef and broccoli, thaw the mixture overnight in the refrigerator and then next day dump the entire thing into a slow cooker. Cook for 6-8 long hours on low or for 3-4 hours.

5) Extract ½ cup of sauce and dissolve the cornstarch in it. Pour the solution all over the beef and vegetables and then cook for another 30 minutes or until the beef and broccoli turns tender enough.

Freezing Instructions:

1) Transfer the cooked beef immediately to a plate or container. Place a lid or cloth loosely on top and refrigerate immediately to cool and avoid contamination. Once cooled, transfer the meat to a freezer ready bag or container and add the remaining ingredients as advised for freezing.

Thawing Instructions:

1) To thaw the food, place the container or bag under running water or alternatively place it in the refrigerator for 12 hours.

Pot Roast Beef

Servings: 4-5

Preparation Time: 15-20 minutes

Cooking Time: 8-10 hours

Ingredients:

2 ½ lbs. (~1.1 kg) of bottom round or chuck roast

1 cup of chopped yellow onion

2 medium sized carrots, peeled and sliced

1 cup of gluten free beef or chicken broth

5 medium sized potatoes, cubed

3 large cloves of garlic, grated or minced

1 tablespoon of extra virgin olive oil

1 tablespoon of gluten free Italian seasoning

2 tablespoons of rice flour or any other gluten free flour

Salt, to taste

Freshly ground black pepper, to taste

Method of preparation:

1) Rinse, peel, cut and slice the carrots, onions, garlic cloves and potatoes. Set those aside. Now take a large and heavy skillet and place it over medium high heat. Grease the skillet with olive oil and once hot enough, place the beef roast in it.
2) Cook until the beef roast is nicely browned on all sides. Set aside when done. Place the browned beef roast in a freezer compatible air tight jar when cooled. Add the chopped and sliced carrots, onions and garlic. Sprinkle the Italian seasoning and then season with salt and black pepper. Stir a bit to mix everything nicely and then pop the container into freezer.

3) Let it stand in freezer and remove it from freezer once you are ready to cook. Let thaw overnight in refrigerator. Dump the beef, potatoes and vegetable mixture into a slow cooker and pour the beef or chicken broth all over it. Place the lid on the slow cooker and let the beef cook on low for 8-10 hours.
4) Ten minutes prior to serving, remove the slow cooker lid and mix the rice flour a little at a time while stirring constantly. Put the lid back and let cook for another 30 minutes.

Freezing Instructions:
1) Cool the browned beef immediately after cooking. Pack in freezer bags or containers to freeze.

Thawing Instructions:
1) Transfer the container to a microwave oven to thaw the food, provided the container is microwave compatible. Don't thaw bags in microwave oven unless otherwise stated.

Beef Stroganoff

Servings: 5-6

Preparation Time: 15-20 minutes

Cooking Time: 8-10 hours

Ingredients:

3 lbs. (~1 kg 360 g) of bone-in chuck roast

1 cup of sour cream

3 cups of gluten free beef broth

2 cups of sliced mushrooms

1 large clove of garlic, chopped

1 bunch of fresh parsley, roughly chopped

3 medium sized yellow or red onion, peeled and diced

Salt, to taste

2 tablespoons of Worcestershire sauce (gluten free)

½ cup of salted butter

3 tablespoons of any gluten free flour

Method of preparation:

1) Rinse the chuck roast thoroughly and cut it into 1 ½ inch sized pieces. Now take the onions, mushrooms, garlic cloves and parsley and rinse those thoroughly under running water. Peel and chop the onion and garlic cloves. Follow that by slicing the mushrooms and chopping the onions.
2) Prepare the slow cooker and drop the butter in it. Then add the chopped garlic, mushrooms and onions. Add-in the beef and then stir-in the Worcestershire sauce, 2 ½ cups of beef broth and salt. Cover and let the beef cook on low for 7-9 hours or on high for 4-5 hours.
3) In the meantime, dissolve the flour in the remaining broth and set aside.

Open the lid of the slow cooker 30 minutes prior to serving the beef stroganoff and pour the broth mixture over the vegetables and beef. Follow that by adding the fresh parsley. Cook for 30 minutes more.

4) Once ready, pack in batches in gallon sized zip lock bags and store in freezer. Take out the bag from the freezer and allow it to thaw in the refrigerator overnight. When thawed completely, return the beef stroganoff in slow cooker and add the sour cream to it. Cook for an additional 5-10 minutes or until heated thoroughly. Serve over gluten free pasta, baked potatoes or warm rice.

Freezing Instructions:

1) Cool down the food completely in the refrigerator before packing in container or freezer zip lock bags.

Thawing Instructions:

1) Place the bag or container under running water or in refrigerator overnight to thaw.

Beef Stew

Servings: 4-5

Preparation time: 15-20 minutes

Cooking time: 8-10 hours

Ingredients:

2 ½ lbs. (~1.1 kg) of beef stew meat

2 cups of gluten free beef broth or water

6 slices of bacon

1 cup of sliced carrots (peeled and sliced)

2-3 shallots, roughly chopped

1 tablespoon of tomato paste (gluten free)

1 tablespoon of herbs de Provence

3 tablespoons of melted butter

1/4th teaspoon of fresh thyme

4-5 large cloves of garlic, peeled and minced

Salt, to taste

Freshly ground black pepper, to taste

Method of preparation:
1) Cut the beef stew meat into medium sized pieces. Peel and chop the carrots and shallots and then mince the cloves of garlic. Once ready, pull out a gallon-sized zip lock bag or air tight container (freezer friendly) and put the beef, carrots, garlic, tomato paste and slices of bacon. Sprinkle the herbs de Provence, fresh thyme, salt and ground black pepper. Give a nice stir or shake to mix the herbs and seasonings with the meats and vegetables and then lock the bag or container.

2) Keep the bag or container in the freezer and take it out to thaw the day before cooking. Thaw in the refrigerator for 12 hours. To cook, pour the

melted butter into the crock pot and then dump the meat and vegetables mixture into the slow cooker. Pour the beef broth or water to cover and cook the meat on low for 8-10 hours or until thoroughly cooked and tender.

Freezing instructions:
1) To freeze the beef stew, pack the suggested ingredients in a freezer specific gallon zip lock bag or an air tight container and pop the container in the freezer to freeze.

Thawing instructions:
1) It is important to thaw the frozen beef properly and safely before cooking it in the slow cooker. For that, the bag or the container should be allowed to sit in the refrigerator for 24 hours.

Garlic Ginger Beef

Servings: 6-8

Preparation time: 15-20 minutes

Cooking time: 7-1/2-8 hours

Ingredients:

4 lbs. (~1.8 kg) of tough cut beef

1 cup of gluten free soy sauce

1 ½ inch of peeled ginger

12 cloves of garlic, peeled

1 lb. (453.592 g) of frozen green beans

3/4th cup of honey or maple syrup

Salt, to taste

Method of preparation:
1) Cut the beef into medium small pieces. Set aside. Peel the garlic cloves and the ginger rhizome. Drop the beef pieces into a freezer safe zip lock bag and then add the ginger rhizome and the garlic cloves to it.

2) Now mix the honey, soy sauce and salt in a bowl and then pour the mixture of over the beef pieces. Close the bag by forcing out the entire or at least most of the air from it and then give a nice toss to mix the ingredients with the beef pieces.

3) Store the bag of beef in the freezer to freezer and thaw it when ready to use. Once thawed, tip the beef mixture into a slow cooker and cook on low for 6 hours. Once the time elapses, pour the thawed beans over the beef. Cook for an additional 90 minutes before serving over warm rice.

Freezing instructions:
1) It is always recommended to use a freezer compatible zip lock bag for freezing food, including beef.

Thawing instructions:
1) To thaw the bag, remove it from the freezer and place it in the refrigerator for 24 hours. Alternatively, place the bag under running water after placing it in the refrigerator for some time to thaw it partially.

Italian Beef Sandwich

Servings: 4-5

Preparation time: 5 minutes

Cooking time: 7-12 hours

Ingredients:

3 lbs. (1 kg 360 g) of bottom round roast beef

2 cups of pepperoncini pepper

2 oz. (~57 g) of dry roast Italian salad dressing mix (gluten free)

1 cup of water

Gluten free bun breads

Method of preparation:

1) Mix the water and Italian salad dressing in a bowl. Add in the peppers and stir to mix together. Drop the bottom round roast beef in a bag and then add the pepper mixture to the beef pieces.

2) Seal the bag tightly and give a nice toss to mix the spices and herbs with beef pieces. Once done, place the beef packet in the freezer to freeze the meat.

3) Place the bag in the refrigerator to thaw the meat and once thawed, cook the beef in the slow cooker for 7-8 hours on high or for 10-12 hours on low. Once ready, serve the meat mixture as sandwich in your choice of gluten free bread.

Freezing instructions:

1) This recipe or food tastes better on freezing. For that, freeze the meat with the rest of the ingredients in a resealable freezing bag.

Thawing instructions:
1) Keep the bag of beef in the refrigerator for 24 hours to thaw the meat and use within 1 hour of thawing or refreeze if not using or in case of any leftovers.

Beef Bourguignon

Servings: 4-5

Preparation time: 1-2 hours

Cooking time: 8-1/2 - 9 1/2 hours

Ingredients:

3 lbs. (1 kg 360 g) of beef stew meat or beef roast

1 large yellow onion, peeled and sliced in rings

2 cups of red wine

6-7 slices or strips of bacon

1 small bunch of thyme

14 oz. (~400 g) of sliced mushrooms

1 cup of sliced carrots

1 tablespoon of tomato paste

2 tablespoons of olive oil

1 teaspoon of Herbs de Provence

3 bay leaves

4 large cloves of garlic, peeled and smashed

A handful of fresh chopped parsley

1 teaspoon of kosher salt

1/2 teaspoon of ground black pepper

Method of preparation:
1) Throw the beef pieces into a bowl and add the wine, bay leaves, a pinch of black pepper and the bunch of thyme to the beef. Stir to combine well and then pop the bowl into the refrigerator to marinade the meat. Let sit for 1-2 hours and then remove the bowl from the refrigerator.

2) Strain the beef pieces from the wine mixture and then set it aside.

Prepare a slow cooker and grease it with the olive oil. Line the chopped onion rings and garlic cloves in the cooker and then place 3 bacon slices on top. Now dump the beef into the cooker and sprinkle the Herbs de Provence on top.

3) Now add the tomato paste and line the remaining bacon strips on the top of the beef pieces. Next, add the sliced capt pieces on top then pour the reserved wine on the top of the beef mixture. Cover and let cook on high for 4-5 hours or on low for 8-9 hours. Freeze the beef recipe if you need at this point, before adding the fried mushrooms.

4) Fry the sliced mushrooms in a skillet in the meantime while the meat is cooking and then add the fried mushroom to the beef 30 minutes prior to complete cooking. Once done, serve over mashed potatoes.

Freezing instructions:
1) Beef bourguignon tastes a lot better frozen than fresh, as the juices then get the time to penetrate the meat pieces and turn them softer and tastier. The cooked beef recipe can be frozen in special air tight jars or zip lock bags, sans the fried mushrooms. This dish will remain good for as long as 3 months. However, make sure to cool the beef immediately before freezing.

Thawing instructions:
1) Thaw the cooked beef mixture as usual in the refrigerator overnight or place in a bowl of water.

Section 4: Lamb

Lamb Tangine

Servings: 5-6

Preparation Time: 15-20 minutes

Cooking Time: 8-10 hours

Ingredients:

2 ½ lbs. (1.1 kg) of lamb shoulder

24 oz. (~710 ml) of gluten free chicken stock

1 teaspoon of paprika

2 teaspoons of ground cumin

2 tablespoons of rice flour (any other gluten free flour)

2 large red onions, sliced

2 teaspoons of ground ginger

3 medium sized carrots, sliced

1 teaspoon of ground cardamom

5 medium sized cloves of garlic, peeled and chopped

1 teaspoon of turmeric

1 large stick of cinnamon

A pinch of saffron strands

2 tablespoons of honey

2 tablespoon of olive oil

1 cup of dried apricots, chopped

2 tablespoons of chopped fresh parsley

12 pitted prunes

1 teaspoon of salt

1 teaspoon of black pepper

Method of preparation:

1) Take a medium sized bowl and tip the rice flour, ground cardamom, paprika, black pepper, ground ginger, salt, saffron, 1 tablespoon of olive oil and turmeric in the bowl. Stir to mix well and then transfer the mixture to a gallon zip lock pouch and add-in the cinnamon stick. Place the lamb in the pouch and toss to combine well.

2) Once ready with the meat, place the bag in the freezer for at least 8-12 hours. Thaw the meat completely by placing it in the refrigerator for at least 12 hours.

3) Take a skillet and place it on medium heat when ready to cook. Slice the onions and carrots in the meantime. Grease the skillet and dump the sliced onions into the skillet.

4) Stir and fry until the onions turn tender and golden brown in color. Once done, dump the fried onions into the slow cooker and place the marinated meat in the skillet to brown. Once browned, transfer the meat to the slow cooker.

5) Add the apricots, prunes, sliced carrots and chopped garlic and cook the meat and vegetables in the slow cooker on low for 8-10 hours or on high for 2-4 hours. Once almost ready, remove the lid and stir-in the rice flour a little at a time until the sauce thickens up. Then add the chopped parsley and honey. Heat for another 10-15 minutes and serve over couscous or rice.

6) Freeze the leftover in freezer gallon zip lock bag. Thaw completely and reheat in slow cooker for 30 minutes to 1 hour on slow.

Freezing Instructions:

1) To freeze the leftover food, let it first cool down in the refrigerator and then freeze in air tight jars or container or sealable bags.

Thawing Instructions: Thaw by refrigerating the bag or container for 12 hours.

Lamb Curry

Servings: 8

Preparation Time: 5-10 minutes

Cooking Time: 8-10 hours

Ingredients:

2 lbs. (~908 g) of boneless lamb (cut into 1 inch sized cubes)

½ cup of yogurt (gluten free)

1 ¾ cups of diced tomatoes

2 tablespoons of rice flour

A pinch of turmeric

1 stick of cinnamon

4 large cloves of garlic, peeled and minced

2 tablespoons of grated fresh ginger

1 teaspoon of crushed black peppercorns

2 teaspoons of paprika

2 teaspoons of garam masala

1-2 tablespoons of cooking oil

2 cups of chopped white onion (finely chopped)

2 teaspoons of ground cumin

½ cup of chopped cilantro (fresh)

Salt, to taste

Method of preparation:
1) Place a large and heavy skillet over medium heat. Pour oil into the skillet and let heat up. Once hot and steaming, dump the lamb pieces into the skillet and brown on all sides.

2) Take the garlic, tomatoes, ginger and onion. Peel the onion and garlic cloves and chop them finely. Peel the ginger as well and grate and chop

the tomatoes. Once the browned meat cools down, transfer it to an air-tight container. Follow that by adding chopped vegetables.

3) Next, add the ground cumin, cinnamon stick, turmeric, paprika, crushed black peppercorns, salt and garam masala to the meat and vegetables in the container. Give a light stir to mix the spices and seasonings with the mixture and keep in the freezer. Take out the container from the freezer a day before cooking and thaw in the refrigerator for 12 hours.

4) To cook the lamb curry, dump everything into the slow cooker and cook it lid-on for 8-10 hours on low. Stir-in the rice flour and yogurt before serving and cook for another 5 minutes in the slow cooker. Finally serve with rice with chopped fresh cilantro.

Freezing Instructions:

1) Place the browned meat on a plate and the plate above ice cold water to cool it after cooking. Pack the cooled meat in container or zip lock bag to freeze.

Thawing Instructions:

1) If stored in a microwave friendly container or bag, thaw the meat in the microwave oven under defrosting menu. Or else, thaw under running water or refrigerator.

Lamb Stew

Servings: 8

Preparation Time: 20-30 minutes

Cooking Time: 8 hours

Ingredients:

2lbs. (~908 g) of lamb, cut into inch sized pieces

3-4 large carrots, peeled and sliced

2 lbs. (~908 g) of small potatoes, peeled and halved

1 3/4th cups of gluten free chicken broth

3 large sized leeks, sliced

2 tablespoons of oil

3 stalks of celery, sliced

2 bay leaves

4 tablespoons of chopped fresh parsley

2 teaspoons of chopped fresh thyme

1 teaspoon of salt

1 teaspoon of ground black pepper

Method of preparation:
1) Clean the leek and other vegetables thoroughly until completely rid of any dirt and grime. Chop the celery stalks, leeks, carrots, potatoes, thyme and parsley as required. Set aside. Grease a crock pot and then dump the lamb cubes into the crock pot.
2) Add the sliced and chopped vegetables, bay leaves, salt, thyme and ground black pepper to the lamb and pour the chicken broth on top to cover. Once done, place the lid on the slow cooker and cook on low for 8-10 hours or until the meat and the other vegetables turn tender. Once prepared, sprinkle the chopped parsley on top and stir well.

3) To freeze the dish, cool it completely and then pour it into a gallon zip lock pouch. Lock the pouch tightly and place it in an air tight container. Place in the freezer until ready to eat. This stew will remain good for 1 month in the freezer. Reheat in the slow cooker for 30 minutes to 1 hour when ready to use.

Freezing Instructions:

1) Cool the stew in the refrigerator before packing in a freezer compatible sealable bag or container to freeze.

Thawing Instructions:

1) To thaw the lamb stew, remove the air tight container from the freezer and place it in the refrigerator for a few hours. Remove the gallon pouch from the container once partly thawed and place it the refrigerator overnight to thaw completely.

Lamb Stew with Peanut Sauce

Servings: 4-5

Preparation time: 30-40 minutes

Cooking time: 6-8 hours

Ingredients:

3 lbs. (1 kg 360 g) of lamb shoulder, fat trimmed and cut into 1 ½ inch sized pieces

1/4th cup of chopped roasted peanuts

3 tablespoons of dark brown sugar

1 large clove of garlic, peeled and minced

1 tablespoon of molasses (gluten free)

3 tablespoons of low sodium and gluten free soy sauce

4 tablespoons of smooth peanut butter

1/8th teaspoon of cayenne pepper powder

2 tablespoons of chopped fresh cilantro

2 tablespoons of olive oil

2 tablespoons of fresh lemon juice

1/4th cup of water

Salt, to taste

Freshly ground black pepper, to taste

Method of preparation:

1) To start, place a skillet over the heat and grease it with the olive oil. Once hot, tip the lamb pieces in the skillet and brown those on all sides nicely. Once done, transfer the browned lamb pieces to the slow cooker with the help of a slotted spoon.

2) Now add the garlic to the skillet and sauté for a minute. Once done, add the

brown sugar, peanut butter, molasses, soy sauce, cayenne pepper and lemon juice to the garlic. Stir around to mix and scrape up the brown bits of lamb. Once the sauce combines, add the water to the sauce and mix well.

3) Once the sauce is prepared, pour it over the lamb pieces in the slow cooker and cook the lamb covered for 6 to 8 hours on low in the slow cooker. Once cooked, cool the food immediately in the fridge and then pack into a sealable bag to freeze.

4) To use, thaw the bag of lamb and tip it into the slow cooker to reheat. Add the chopped peanuts at this point of time and adjust the seasoning as well. Once ready, serve hot by garnishing with the chopped cilantro.

Freezing instructions:
1) Freezing this recipe after cooking makes the lamb taste better and in order to do so, cool the cooked lamb immediately by placing to in the refrigerator. Once thoroughly cooked, pack the lamb in a bag or jar with having airtight facility and freeze by marking the container or pouch.

Thawing instructions:
1) Remove the frozen lamb 24 hours before cooking from the freezer and place it in the refrigerator for 24 hours to thaw completely.

Lamb Shank

Servings: 8-10

Preparation time: 30-40 minutes

Cooking time: 6 -8 hours

Ingredients:

8.8 lbs. (4 kg) of lamb shanks

2 medium sized carrots, peeled and chopped

1 cup of red wine

2 medium onions, peeled and chopped

2 cups of low sodium beef stock, gluten free

2 tablespoons of tomato paste

1/2 cup of corn flour

1.76 lbs. (~800 grams) of chopped tomatoes

1 bouquet garni

4 large clove of garlic, peeled and smashed

2 tablespoons of sugar

2 tablespoons of olive oil

Method of preparation:

1) Place a frying pan on heat and use 1 tablespoon of olive oil to grease it. Once hot, toss the lamb pieces in a mixture of salt, ground black pepper and corn flour and then brown those in the oil. Once browned, dump into the slow cooker.

2) Add the remaining oil to the frying pan and toss the garlic and onion in it. Stir and cook the onion and garlic until they start to soften and then add the tomato paste to it. Stir and cook for a few more minutes and then deglaze the pan with the wine.

3) Scrape up the brown bits of meat and then let the sauce come to a boil. Follow that by adding the beef stock, sugar, chopped tomatoes and the bouquet garni. Boil and cook for 5 minutes on medium low heat and then dump over the lamb in the slow cooker.

4) Cook the lamb covered on high for 6-8 hours or until the lamb turns soft and starts falling apart from the bone. Once that happens, take out the lamb pieces from the slow cooker and set aside in the fridge to cool.

5) Cook the sauce uncovered for another 30 minutes to thicken it up and then store it separately in the fridge to cool. Once both the lamb and the sauce cools down completely, transfer the lamb and the sauce in a gallon zip lock bash which is freezer compatible and then pop the labeled packet into the freezer to freeze. Use as and when needed and thaw completely before reheating.

Freezing instructions:

1) It is important to cool down the lamb and the sauce before freezing so as to avoid ruining their taste and to keep them safer. Discard the bouquet garni before freezing.

Thawing instructions:

1) Thaw the bag of lamb as usually in the refrigerator 24 hours prior to cooking.

Lamb and Fig Stew

Servings: 6-8

Preparation time: 10 minutes

Cooking time: 7-9 hours

Ingredients:

1 ½ lbs. (~680 g) of boneless lamb leg or shoulder, trimmed of excess fat and cubed

1 cup of dried figs, stemmed and halved

1 lb. (~450 g) of red onions, peeled and cut in wedges

1 ½ lbs. (~680 g) of sweet potatoes, peeled and cubed

2 cups of low sodium chicken broth, gluten free

1 tablespoon of grated orange peel

2 cups of dry white wine

4 tablespoons of corn flour

1/2 cup of dry white wine

1/2 cup of minced parsley

Salt, to taste

Ground black pepper, to taste

Method of preparation:

1) Tip the lamb pieces, 2 cups of white wine, beef broth, grated orange peel, sweet potato cubes and onion wedges into the slow cooker. Cover and cook the lamb on low for 6-8 hours or until the lamb turns tender.

2) Once cooked, cool the lamb in the refrigerator and then freeze it by packing it in a freezer safe zip lock resealable bag. To use the lamb, thaw the bag and then tip the contents of the bag into the slow cooker.

3) Add the fig and dissolve the corn flour in the remaining wine. Add both the fig and the corn flour slurry to the lamb and then cook it for an additional 45 minutes. Serve with the chopped parsley.

Freezing instructions:
1) The lamb must be thoroughly cooled before freezing.

Thawing instructions:
1) Thawing should be ideally done by placing frozen lamb in the fridge for 24 hours.

Slow Roasted Leg of Lamb

Servings: 6-8

Preparation time: 10-12 hours

Cooking time: 8 hours

Ingredients:

2 lbs. +12 oz. (1.25 kg) leg of lamb, without shank

10-12 tablespoons of olive oil

3-4 cups of roughly chopped fresh mint

7-8 cloves of garlic, peeled and smashed

2-3 sprigs of fresh rosemary

Salt

Method of preparation:

1) Prepare a rub by my mixing the rosemary, smashed garlic and mint leaves with the olive oil. Season with salt.

2) Rub the herb mix all over the lamb and then keep the lamb in the refrigerator overnight or for at least a few hours by covering it with foil.

3) Once ready to cook, remove the lamb from the fridge and prepare a skillet on medium heat. Oil the skillet sufficiently and then brown the lamb in that.

4) Once properly browned on all sides, tip the browned lamb pieces into a slow cooker and cook on low for 8 hours.

5) Cool the lamb immediately once cooked and then freeze in freezer compatible container.

Freezing instructions:

    1)   Slow roasted lamb will stay good for as long as 3-4 days when properly frozen in good quality containers. It is important to cool the meat immediately by placing it in the fridge before packing to freeze.

Thawing instructions:

    1)   Lamb legs should be thoroughly thawed before reheating. Use the reheated left over within 1 hour. Place in refrigerator for 24 hours prior to reheating.

Chapter 4: Rice and Casseroles

Chicken Broccoli Rice Casserole

Servings: 3-4

Preparation Time: 30-40 minutes

Cooking Time: 40-50 minutes

Ingredients:

6 cups of cooked basmati rice

5 cups of cooked chicken (chicken breasts or thighs)

1-1/2 cups of whole milk

2/3rd cup of softened salted butter

3 heads of broccoli

2 cups of sliced mushrooms (any variety)

16 oz. (453.592 g) of shredded Cheddar cheese

1 teaspoon of garlic powder

1 teaspoon of salt

Method of preparation:
1) Cook the basmati rice so that you have 6 cups worth of cooked rice. Cook the chicken alongside and then shred the chicken. Now take 3 freezer friendly sealable bags and grease those with oil or cooking spray. Once done, set aside.
2) Wash and slice the mushrooms and chop the heads of garlic. Add those along with the broccoli, salt, shredded chicken and garlic powder. Mix and pack into a freezer container bag.
3) Once ready to use, drop the butter in the crock pot and then dump the rice mixture in. Add-in the milk and mix well until well absorbed. Once done, add-in half of the cheese and cook on low for 6 hours or until the

entire cheese is melted.

4) Once ready, spread the remaining shredded cheese over the rice mixture in the baking pans. Cook the casserole for 5-10 minutes more and serve warm.

Freezing Instructions:

1) Casseroles taste better when frozen and stay as long as 3-4 months if properly frozen. To freeze this casserole, pack the rice and vegetables, except the milk and cheese in freezer bags or containers and freeze in small batches for convenience.

Thawing Instructions:

1) Thaw in microwave oven in defrost setting or refrigerator for 12 hours.

Southwestern Casserole

Servings: 7-8

Preparation Time: 10-15 minutes

Cooking Time: 6-8 hours

Ingredients:

1 cup of brown rice, uncooked

1 lb. (~455 g) of ground beef

1/2 cup of frozen corn

1 1/4th cup of chopped red onion

4 cups of soaked kidney beans

1 cup of shredded cheddar cheese

14-1/2 oz. (411.068 g) diced red tomatoes

2 teaspoons of chili powder

1 ½ cups of chopped green pepper

1/4th cup of water

2 tablespoons of chopped fresh cilantro

1 teaspoon of cumin

1 cup of gluten free ketchup

Method of preparation:
1) Soak the kidney beans in water overnight. When ready to cook, take a gallon size freezer compatible zip lock pouch and dump the rice in it. To the rice, add the beef, diced tomatoes, frozen corn, chopped green pepper, soaked kidney beans, chopped onion and chopped cilantro.
2) Follow that by adding the ketchup, ground cumin and chili powder. Once everything is added, take a small zip lock bag and store the cheese in it. Insert the small bag into the gallon zip lock bag and then seal the

gallon pouch.

3) Label and insert the pouch into the freezer. Thaw the bags separately in the refrigerator overnight before cooking and then dump the contents of the bag into the slow cooker. Top with water and cook on low for 6-8 hours or until the rice is thoroughly cooked. Once done, top with the shredded cheese before serving.

Freezing Instructions:

1) Use freezer ready zip lock bags or containers to pack the casserole and freeze it.

Thawing Instructions:

1) Thaw completely by placing the bag or container under running water; in refrigerator for 12 hours or in microwave oven if using microwave proof container or bag.

Crockpot Fried Rice

Servings: 4-6

Preparation Time: 15 minutes

Cooking Time: 3-4 hours

Ingredients:

2 cups of cooked rice (normal or brown rice)

1/2 cup of fresh peas

2 teaspoons of gluten free Worcestershire sauce

2 eggs

1/4th cup of diced carrots

1/2 yellow onion, peeled and chopped

1/4th cup of chopped celery

1 ½ cups of cooked chicken

2 tablespoons of gluten free soy sauce

Salt, to taste

3 tablespoons of salted butter

Sesame seeds, for serving

Method of preparation:
1) Wash all the raw vegetables and then peel and chop the onion. Follow that by chopping the celery and carrots. Once done, take a gallon sized zip lock pouch or freezer compatible air tight jar. Spread the cooked rice, chicken and the chopped vegetables. Add-in the soy sauce and Worcestershire sauce and then give a nice stir to the rice. Once everything is mixed, pop the jar or container or pouch into the freezer and let relax.
2) Take out the jar from the freezer on the day of cooking and thaw the

rice completely. Prepare the slow cooker by dropping the butter in it. Empty the contents of the jar or bag into the slow cooker and then let the rice cook for 3-4 hours on low or for 2-3 hours on high.

3) In the meantime, fry the egg in a pan and spread it over the rice half an hour before serving. Garnish with sesame seeds and serve warm.

Freezing Instructions:

1) Spread the rice loosely in a container and lock it to freeze.

Thawing Instructions:

1) Remove from freezer and place in the refrigerator for 12 hours to thaw the rice before cooking.

Western Beef Casserole

Servings: 4

Preparation time: 20 minutes

Cooking time: 4 hours

Ingredients:

1-½ lb. (680 g) of lean beef, grounded

1 cup of sharp cheddar cheese, shredded

4 tablespoons of milk or water

1 and 1/16 oz. (30 g) can of gluten free kidney beans, drained and rinsed

1 medium sized yellow onion, peeled and chopped

1 and 1/16 oz. (30 g) can of gluten free corns, drained and washed

1 and 1/10.75 oz. (~32 ml) of gluten free tomato soup

1/8th teaspoon of red chili powder

Method of preparation:

1) Brown the grounded beef in a skillet and cool immediately in refrigerator. Once cooled, transfer the meat to a gallon zip lock bag and then add the corns, kidney beans, tomato soup, chili powder and chopped onions to the beef.

2) Lock the bag and give a nice stir or shake to the bag to mix all the ingredients nicely with the beef. Lock tightly and pop into the freezer to freeze.

3) Thaw the bag of beef and transfer the ingredients of the bag to the slow cooker. Add the milk and the cheddar cheese to the meat mixture. Give a light stir to mix and then cook on low for 4 hours or on high for 1-2 hours.

Freezing instructions:

1) Freeze the beef mixture in a zip lock bag or container that is air tight and freezer safe. Cool the beef immediately in fridge after cooking.

Thawing instructions:

1) Transfer the bag of beef from the freezer to the fridge to thaw the packet of beef

Pizza Casserole

Servings: 3-4

Preparation time: 20-30 minutes

Cooking time: 4-5 hours

Ingredients:

1 box of gluten free spiral pasta, uncooked

1 large green bell pepper, chopped

1 lb. (~455 g) of lean ground turkey

1 cup of mozzarella cheese, shredded

1 large yellow onion, peeled and chopped

½ cup of water

2 cups of gluten free pasta or pizza sauce (preferably homemade)

1 cup of pepperoni or bacon

2 large cloves of garlic, peeled and chopped

½ can of pitted olives

Method of preparation:

1) Prepare the meal by browning the turkey with the onion, bell pepper and garlic. Once browned, transfer to fridge to cool immediately.

2) Once cooled, transfer the turkey mixture to a sturdy zip lock bag and add the pasta or pizza sauce, olives and pepperoni to the turkey mixture and freeze.

3) Thaw the bag of turkey when ready to cook and tip the turkey mixture to a greased slow cooker. Add boiled pasta and the water to the beef mixture. Top with shredded mozzarella cheese. Cook covered on low for 4-5 hours.

Freezing instructions:

1) The cooked turkey mixture should be thoroughly cooled in the refrigerator before freezing.

Thawing instructions:

1) Place the bag in the refrigerator for 24 hours to thaw the turkey mixture.

Squash Casserole

Servings: 8-10

Preparation time: 20 minutes

Cooking time: 2 hours

Ingredients:

9 cups of sliced yellow squash

1 cup of sharp cheddar cheese, shredded

1 tablespoon of butter

1 medium sized onion, peeled and chopped

2/3rd cup of sour cream

2 cups of gluten free bread crumbs

1 tablespoon of melted butter

½ teaspoon of garlic salt

A handful of chopped freshly parsley

2 3/4th cup of cream of chicken soup

1/4th teaspoon of ground black pepper

Method of preparation:

1) Microwave the squash and onion with butter until tender. Drain all the liquid. Grease a slow cooker nicely and mix the squash mixture with 1 cup breadcrumbs, garlic salt, soup, ½ cup of cheese, sour cream, black pepper and garlic salt.

2) Mix remaining bread crumbs with remaining cheese and melted butter. Crumble the mixture and spread it over the casserole. Cover and cook for 2 hours on low. Refrigerate to cool and cover with aluminum foil to freeze. Thaw in microwave oven to serve later.

Freezing instructions:

1) Use an air tight container to freeze the cooled squash casserole. Place an aluminum foil on top before freezing.

Thawing instructions:

1) Thaw for 24 hours in refrigerator or defrost in microwave before reheating.

Chapter 5: Desserts

Molten Choco Lava Cake

Servings: 6-8

Preparation Time: 30-40 minutes

Cooking Time: 1-2 hours

Ingredients:

1 ½ cups of almond flour

1/3rd cup of gluten free brown sugar

1 cup of gluten free sugar (2/3rd cup+ 1/3rd cup separated)

1 ½ cups of hot water

1/3rd cup of whole milk

1/3rd cup + 3 tablespoons of gluten free cocoa powder

1 egg yolk (preferably organic)

1/3rd cup of chocolate chips (gluten free)

7 tablespoons of salted butter

1 tablespoon of vanilla extracts (gluten free)

2 teaspoons of baking powder

Method of preparation:

1) Take a medium sized bowl and tip the almond flour in it. Add the baking powder and whisk briefly. Set aside. Take a microwave safe bowl and tip 6 tablespoons of butter in it. Add the chocolate chips to the butter. Give a light stir to mix and insert in the microwave oven to melt the mixture.

2) Once melted, add the milk, 2/3rd cup of sugar, vanilla extract, cocoa powder and the almond flour and baking powder mixture to the molten chocolate mixture. Stir to combine well and then set aside the batter.

3) Grease the inside of the crockpot with the remaining butter and then

pour the prepared batter into the crockpot. Take another bowl and combine the brown sugar, remaining 1/3rd cup of sugar and the cocoa powder in it. Once thoroughly combined, pour the mixture over the batter in the crockpot.

4) Put the lid on the crockpot and cook on high for 1-2 hours or until the sides of the cake starts pulling off from the crockpot. The top will stay liquid. Once done, remove from the crockpot and let cool down for 15 minutes before serving.

Freezing instructions:

1) This cake will freeze nice after the batter is made. For that, pour the batter into a baking pan, without the chocolate mixture on top and cover with two coats of cling film. These will stay good for as long as 1 month.

Thawing instructions:

1) Remove from freezer and thaw completely in refrigerator overnight. When ready to use, remove the wrap, pour chocolate mixture on top and cook in slow cooker 1-2 hours more or until the desired consistency is achieved.

Orange Cheesecake

Servings: 10

Preparation Time: 25-30 minutes

Cooking Time: 2 ½ hours

Ingredients:

1 ½ tablespoon of almond flour

12 oz. (~340 g) of reduced fat cream cheese, softened

½ cup of sour cream

½ cup of gluten free sugar

3 large eggs

1 teaspoon of shredded orange peel

1 cup of warm water

2 tablespoons of fresh or gluten free packaged orange juice

½ teaspoon of vanilla extract

1 medium orange, horizontally sliced

Method of Preparation:
1) Take a heavy foil and cut it in half lengthwise. Fold the foil into thirds and repeat the same with some more foils. Once ready, criss-cross the folded foils to make a lattice. Take a casserole dish and spray it with cooking spray to grease. Place the greased casserole dish over the lattice.
2) Take a large bowl and drop the softened cream cheese in it. Add the almond flour, sugar, vanilla extract and the orange juice to it, beat on medium speed until combined and then add-in the sour cream and the eggs. Better if 1 egg is combined at a time. Beat until just combined.
3) Once ready, pour the mixture into the casserole dish and cover with a foil. Now fill up a slow cooker with warm water and transfer the

casserole dish with the foil lattice affixed underneath into the slow cooker. Let cook for 2 ½ hours or until set. Once ready, remove from slow cooker and cool completely.

4) Once cooled, cover with a cling film and transfer the cheesecake into the freezer. Freeze for as long as 1 month. To use, thaw and serve with orange slices.

Freezing Instructions:

1) Cover with a cling film to freeze the cheesecake for 24 hours to 1 month.

Thawing Instructions:

1) To use the cheesecake, let it sit in refrigerator overnight before using and use within 2 days once thawed.

Low Fat Carrot Cake

Servings: 12

Preparation Time: 45-50 minutes

Cooking Time: 2 ½ - 3 ½ hours

Ingredients:

1 3/4th cups of almond flour

1 cup of fresh grated carrots

2 large eggs

1 teaspoon of baking powder

1 cup of sugar

1 teaspoon of ground cinnamon

4 tablespoons of water

1 teaspoon of pure vanilla extract

1/3rd cup of vegetable oil

½ teaspoon of baking soda

Cream cheese or whipped cream for frosting

Method of Preparation:
1) Rinse and peel the carrots thoroughly. Grate the carrots and set aside. In a large bowl, tip the vegetable oil and sugar and cream the two together. Add the water and one egg at a time and beat.
2) Once ready, add-in the flour a little at a time and whisk slowly. Combine all the flour and then then add-in the ground cinnamon, baking powder, baking soda and the vanilla extract. Whisk until everything is nicely combined. Finally, fold-in the grated carrots.
3) Grease the inside of the crockpot with oil or cooking spray and pour the entire batter into the crockpot. Put the lid on the slow cooker and cook uninterrupted on slow for 2 ½ - 3 ½ hours or until a skewer comes out

neat even when poked into the center of the cake.

4) Once ready, remove the cake from the crockpot and place it over a wire rack to let it cool down. Once cooled thoroughly, pack the cake with a foil to freeze it.

5) When ready to use, thaw the cake and spread whipped cream or cream cheese on top to serve.

Freezing Instructions:

1) To freeze the cake, wrap the cake or its slices with saran wrap first and then with an aluminum foil before popping it into the freezer. It will stay good for as long as 3 months when packed properly.

Thawing Instructions:

1) Thawing the cake is necessary prior to serving it. For that, remove it from the freezer and let it stand in the refrigerator overnight. Frost the cake after thawing to serve and consume within 2-3 days after thawing.

Peanut Butter Cake

Servings: 4

Preparation time: 30-40 minutes

Cooking time: 2-4 hours

Ingredients:

1 1/4th cup of almond flour (sifted)

½ cup of milk (whole)

1 cup of white granulated sugar

1 cup of boiling water

½ cup of creamy peanut butter (gluten free)

1 teaspoon of baking powder

3 tablespoons of unsweetened cocoa powder (gluten free)

1 tablespoon of vegetable oil

½ teaspoon of sea salt

1 teaspoon of pure vanilla extracts (gluten free)

Method of preparation:

1) Grease the inside of slow cooker with cooking spray. Take a large mixing bowl and tip the sifted flour, baking powder, ½ cup of sugar and the sea salt in it. Give a nice stir to mix well and set aside.

2) Take the peanut butter in a microwave safe bowl and insert it into the microwave to melt. Add the melted peanut butter to the flour mixture. Follow that by adding the oil, milk and vanilla extract.

3) Stir nicely to mix all the liquid ingredients nicely with the dry ingredients and then pour the batter into a 4-quart slow cooker.

4) Now mix the cocoa powder with the remaining ½ cup of sugar and ½ cup of boiling water. Stir to mix well, so that the mixture becomes lump free and then pour the cocoa mixture over the batter in the crock pot.

5) Cover and cook the cake on low for 2-4 hours or until it sets and a toothpick when inserted at the center comes out clean. Once ready, serve as required or cool immediately. Wrap the entire cake or small pieces of it in a saran wrap and store in an air-tight container. Thaw and use as needed.

Freezing instructions:

1) The cake remains just perfect in the freezer and can be used for as long as 1-2 months when frozen properly in saran wrap and container.

Thawing instructions:

1) To thaw the cake, place it for 24 hours in the refrigerator.

Blueberry Crisp

Servings: 4-6

Preparation time: 10 minutes

Cooking time: 3-5 hours

Ingredients:

16 oz. (~455 g) of organic frozen blueberries (gluten free)

1/4th cup of honey

½ cup of chopped pecan

1 cup of gluten free oats

5 tablespoons of softened butter

1.2 cup of almond meal

½ teaspoon of salt

Method of preparation:

1) Stir almond meal, oats and chopped pecans lightly in a bowl to mix. Mix the honey and softened butter to the dry mixture to crumble. Drop the frozen blueberries in a greased slow cooker and then pour the crumbled mixture over the blueberries.

2) Do not press the crumbled mixture and then cook the dessert covered on low for 3-5 hours. Once ready, cool immediately and tip into a zip lock bag to freeze. Thaw to use and serve with a scoop of vanilla ice cream.

Freezing instructions:

1) Refrigerate the warm dessert immediately after cooking to cool it down. Dump the cooled dessert in a zip lock bag and freeze.

Thawing instructions:

1) Thaw the bag of dessert in a refrigerator for 24 hours.

Triple Chocolate Brownies

Servings: 12-14

Preparation time: 40-45 minutes

Cooking time: 4 hours

Ingredients:

2 cups of almond flour

1 cup of chopped bittersweet chocolate

4 tablespoons of unsweetened cocoa powder

3 large eggs

3/4th teaspoon of baking powder

6 oz. (170 g) of semi-sweet gluten free chocolate chips

1/2 cup of unsalted butter

1 cup of white granulated sugar

1 cup of chopped walnut

1/2 teaspoon of sea salt

Method of preparation:

    1) Lightly grease a parchment paper and the base of a slow cooker. Place the greased parchment paper in the greased slow cooker. Mix the almond flour, baking powder, cocoa powder and salt in a bowl. Keep aside.

    2) Melt the chopped chocolate and butter in microwave and then stir-in the eggs, sugar, chocolate chips and the chopped walnuts. Stir lightly to mix and then pour into the parchment paper lined slow cooker.

    3) Cook lid-on for 3-1/2 hours on low and then without lid for an

additional 30 minutes. The center should be still soft and wobbly. Once done, store in fridge to cool and then wrap up the entire thing or the pieces in saran wrap and then store the pieces in air tight containers to freeze.

Freezing instructions:

1) It is best to use saran wrap and a freezer compatible container to store the brownies. Brownies remain good for 3-4 months when stored properly and frozen at constant 0 degrees.

Thawing instructions:

1) To thaw, simply place the brownie in the refrigerator for 24 hours.

Blueberry Cobbler

Servings: 5-6

Preparation time: 45-55 minutes

Cooking time: 2½ hours

Ingredients:

1 cup of almond flour

2 cups of whole frozen blueberries

1-1/4th cup of sugar, divided

1/4th teaspoon of ground nutmeg

4 tablespoons of sour cream

2 large eggs

1/4th cup of water

1/4th teaspoon of ground cinnamon

1 teaspoon of baking powder

3 teaspoons of fresh lemon juice, divided

Method of preparation:

1) Whisk together the almond flour, baking powder, ground cinnamon, 1/4th cup of sugar and the ground nutmeg. Then add the eggs, water, 1 teaspoon of lemon juice and the sour cream. Whisk to combine well and prepare a smooth batter.

2) Mix the frozen blueberries, remaining sugar and remaining lemon juice in another bowl. Set aside. Pour the prepared batter into the slow cooker and dump the blueberry mixture over that. Cook lid-on on low for 2-1/2 hours and then serve warm with a scoop of cream.

3) Store the leftovers in the freezer by packing the cooked cobbler in

a air right container. Thaw and reheat in slow cooker or oven until the crust attains a brown color and serve to use later.

Freezing instructions:

1) Cover the container of cobbler with aluminum foil and then place the lid on top to freeze. Blueberry cobbler stays usable till 3-4 months of preparation. It is also important to cool the cobbler in fridge before freezing.

Thawing inductions:

1) Remove from freezer and let sit in refrigerator for 24 hours.

Recommended Reading For You:

You may also want to check my other books:

Gluten-Free Vegan Cookbook: 90+ Healthy, Easy and Delicious Recipes for Vegan Breakfasts, Salads, Soups, Lunches, Dinners and Desserts

90+ Healthy, Easy and Delicious Recipes for Vegan Breakfasts, Salads, Soups, Lunches, Dinners and Desserts for Your Well-Being + Shopping List to Save Your Precious Time!

Gluten-Free Vegan diet doesn't have to be bland and boring at all! These recipes are original, easy to make and just delightfully appetizing. They will enrich your culinary experience and let you enjoy your breakfasts, lunches, dinners and desserts with your friends and family.

In this book you will find:

-23 Scrumptious and Easy Breakfasts

-27 Delicious and Savory Lunches and Dinners

-22 Aromatic And Nutritious Soups

-21 Enticing And Rich Desserts

-Extra Shopping List to Save Your Precious Time

= 93 Fantastic Gluten-Free Healthy Vegan Recipes!

The Gluten-Free diet will help you detoxify, improve your immune system and make you feel younger - both mentally and physically! The

Change is just in front of you!

->**Direct Buy Link:** http://www.amazon.com/dp/B00LU915YA/

->**Paperback Version:** https://www.createspace.com/4907669

Paleo Smoothie Recipes: 67 Delicious Paleo Smoothies For Weight Loss And a Healthy Lifestyle

67 Easy and Fast Delicious Smoothie Recipes for Effective Weight Loss and Sexy Body!

Kill the food cravings and get in shape with these delicious and healthy Paleo Smoothies!

In This Book I'll Show You:

-Why Paleo Smoothies are great for Weight Loss (and Weight Maintenance!)

-67 Tasty Paleo Recipes great for Weight Loss, Detox, and keeping your body Healthy every day!

-How to make the Paleo approach easier!

-Important facts about some of the ingredients you'd like to know.

-Planning and Directions – how to get started fast!

-How to maintain your motivation, finally lose the extra pounds and be happy with a Sexy Body!

->**Direct Buy Link:** http://www.amazon.com/dp/B00J8ZHMIQ/

->**Paperback Version:** https://www.createspace.com/4803901

Gluten Free Crock Pot Recipes: 59 Healthy, Easy and Delicious Slow Cooker Paleo Recipes for Breakfast, Lunch and Dinner

Discover Healthy, Easy and Delicious Slow Cooker Paleo Recipes for Breakfast, Lunch and Dinner for You and Your Family!

Save your time and start healthy living with these delectable slow cooker gluten free recipes tailor-made for busy people!

I've been on the Gluten Free diet for more than ten years now!

Although the main reason for my radical diet change was my diagnosis (Coeliac disease), I would never-ever (even if given a magical chance) take the lane of eating gluten again!

->**Direct Buy Link:** http://www.amazon.com/dp/B00K5UVYUA/

->**Paperback Version:** https://www.createspace.com/4823966

Low Carb Slow Cooker: 50 Delicious, Fast and Easy Crock Pot Recipes for Rapid Weight Loss

Start Losing Weight Effectively and For Good!

The recipes mentioned in this eBook are not only simple but they require every day ingredients from your kitchen.

Food tastes best when you cook it with some love. Nothing can beat the mouth-watering dishes that can be cooked in a slow cooker.

If you often find yourself confused about how to whip up a yummy dish for a low-carb diet, this eBook is just the perfect thing you need right now.

In This Book You Will Read About:

-What is Low Carb Diet?

-Who Should Use it And Who Should Not?

-Pros and Properties of Low Carb Diet

-Some Common Low Carb Myths

-Best and Worst Food Choices You Can Make

-Foods You Need to Avoid

-Important Tips and Advice

-10 Low-Carb Slow-Cooker Aromatic Soups Recipes

-11 Low-Carb Crockpot Delicious Chicken recipes

-10 Low-carb Slow-cooker Amazingly Good Sea-food

-10 Low-carb slow-cooker Yummy Pork Recipes

-9 Low-carb Slow-cooker Scrumptious Lamb Recipes

->**Direct Buy Link:** http://www.amazon.com/dp/B00O2AACR0/

-> **Paperback Version:** https://www.createspace.com/5042178

Pressure Cooker Recipes: Are You Busy? 65 Fast and Easy Pressure Cooking Ideas to Prepare Scrumptious Meals in No Time!

65 Easy and Scrumptious Pressure Cooker Recipes that Can Be Prepared In Under 20 Minutes! Tender Meats, Aromatic Sauces, Appetizing Bouillons, Delightful Veggies, Savory Soups, Tempting Desserts - It's All Here!

I'm a huge wellness lifestyle aficionado... **but also a working mum.** Although my diet is gluten-free (I'm coeliac) and often vegan, I'm married with kids. I do everything to provide them with varied and delicious diet. **This is my first book which aims at "regular", everyday recipes for busy people who don't follow any diet in particular.**

Since **you don't have too many time on your hands when you're working 9-5** and also maintaining your own diet, **this book's focus is on pressure cooker recipes.** This sweet little device will allow you to prepare **delicious and healthy meals in no time** – although slow cooker is nice to have, pressure cooker is something I definitely couldn't live without.

Pressure Cooker Allows You To Save Huge Amounts of Time! Discover These Enjoyable Recipes And Stop Spending So Much Time in the Kitchen!

Majority of meals in this book can be prepared in under 20 minutes – **there's pork, beef, poultry, fish, seafood, soups, sauces, bouillons, desserts and vegetable meals** – all these scrumptious eats of my choosing that my family loves and keeps asking for!

->**Direct Buy Link:** http://www.amazon.com/dp/B00R0FQMJQ/

->**Paperback Version:** https://www.createspace.com/5180764

DIY HouseHold Hacks: 155 Hacks and Strategies: Clean Your Home Like a Pro: Your Guide On How To Save Massive Time, Energy and Money & Make Life Easier ... (Do It Yourself!)

Clean Your Home Like a Pro! Learn How To Save Your Time, Energy and Money, Stop Using Expensive & Toxic Shop Cleaners! - 155 great hacks and strategies + 41 effective recipes!

What prompted me to go all natural and make my own recipes, is the fact that commercial products these days are **not only expensive, but also laden with so many chemicals. They end up doing more harm than good.** It was; therefore, imperative to **make skin and pet friendly cleaning products at home**, to safeguard my family's health, while **saving massive money and time simultaneously.**

This book is full of proven hacks and interesting ideas that will cut short the time you spend cleaning your house; time that you can spend with family and friends.

Not only will the recipes and hacks help you save on money and energy, they also give you the satisfaction of having done your bit for the conservation of the environment. **You will be surprised how many effective, cheap and harmless cleaning products you already own in your household!**

In This Book You Will Find:

-Easy Bathroom Cleaning Hacks
-Kitchen Cleaning Hacks
-Living room/Hall Cleaning Hacks
-Bedroom Cleaning Hacks
-DIY for your Garden
-Shopping List/Index
-LOTS of tricks, tips & great and easy recipes!

All the hacks and recipes mentioned in the book have been personally tested and the results have always been great!

->**Direct Buy Link:** http://www.amazon.com/dp/B00O4ILFIK/

->**Paperback Version:** https://www.createspace.com/5052647

Anti Inflammatory Diet: Beginner's Guide: What You Need To Know To Heal Yourself with Food + Recipes + One Week Diet Plan

"He who takes medicine and neglects to diet wastes the skill of his doctors."
-Chinese Proverb

Are you suffering from the severe symptoms that you've been trying to overcome for a long time now using your prescribed pills, but just stuck somewhere in the middle?

Unrestrained inflammation lead to asthma, allergies, tissue and cell degeneration, heart diseases, cancer and various other maladies, which are difficult to deal with.
I myself suffered from long and gruesome periods of acute inflammation. I had the IBS symptoms and very bad, extremely painful sinusitis. It started to affect my day to day ability to work and my potential and productivity suffered a steep decline. Medication helped but the effect was only temporary. I would be confined to my house for days without any solution to my problem. Every doctor I visited could pinpoint the superficial problem and treat it but none could tell me what was causing this problem, time after time.

And the problem was my diet!

Vast majority of the recipes I included in this book can be prepared really fast and easily! I also included absolutely delicious One Week Diet Plan for you!

->Direct Buy Link: http://www.amazon.com/dp/B00MQ9HI58/

->Paperback Version: https://www.createspace.com/4974692

You may also want to download my friend's books.

Help your mind today with these:

- Buddhism: Beginner's Guide:

http://www.amazon.com/dp/B00MHSR5YM/

- Meditation: Beginner's Guide:

http://www.amazon.com/ dp/B00KQRU9BC/

- Zen: Beginner's Guide:

http://www.amazon.com/dp/B00PWUBSEK/

My Mailing list: If you would like to receive new Kindle reads on weight loss, wellness, diets, recipes and healthy living for FREE I invite you to my Mailing List. Whenever my new book is out, I set the free period for two days. You will get an e-mail notification and will **be the first to get the book for $0** during its limited promotion.

Why would I do this when it took me countless hours to write these e-books? First of all, that's my way of saying **"thank you"** to my new readers. Second of all – **I want to spread the word about my new books and ideas.** Mind you that **I hate spam and e-mails that come too frequently** - no worries about that.

If you think that's a good idea and are in, just follow this link:
http://eepurl.com/6elQD

You can also follow us on Facebook:

www.facebook.com/HolisticWellnessBooks

We have created this page with a few fellow authors of mine. We hope you find it inspiring and helpful.

Thank You for your time and interest in our work!

Annette Goodman & Holistic Wellness eBooks

About The Author

Hello! My name is Annette Goodman.

I'm glad we met. Who am I?

A homegrown cook, successful wellness aficionado and a writer. I live in Portland, Oregon with my husband, son and our dear golden retriever, Fluffy. I work as a retail manager in of the European companies.

My entire childhood I suffered from obesity, hypertension and complexion problems. During my college years I decided to turn my life around and started my weight-loss and wellness pursue. After more than a decade I can say that I definitely succeeded and now I'd like to give you a hand.

I love creating new healthy recipes, cooking and writing books about healthy lifestyle for you to enjoy and profit from.

I hope we'll meet again!

Visit my Amazon author page:

http://www.amazon.com/Annette-Goodman/e/B00LLPE1QM/

Printed in Great Britain
by Amazon.co.uk, Ltd.,
Marston Gate.